CW01025085

The Barn Garden
Making a Place

Tom and Sue Stuart-Smith

Including photographs by
Marianne Majerus and Andrew Lawson

Published in 2011 by Serge Hill Books
The Barn, Serge Hill, Abbots Langley, Herts WD5 0RY

Text copyright © Tom and Sue Stuart-Smith 2011
Photographic copyright © Marianne Majerus, Andrew Lawson and Stuart-Smith
images, as attributed in the acknowledgments. 2011
All photographs reproduced in this book have permission of the copyright holders.

All rights reserved. This publication may not be reproduced, stored in a retrieval
system or transmitted in any form by any means,
electronic, mechanical, photocopying, recording or otherwise,
without formal permission in writing from the publisher.

Cover photograph by Marianne Majerus
Design by Luca Puri
Typset in Franklin Gothic Book
Printed throughout on Hello Silk
Printed and bound in the UK by Hampton Printing (Bristol) Ltd

ISBN 978-0-9568640-0-0

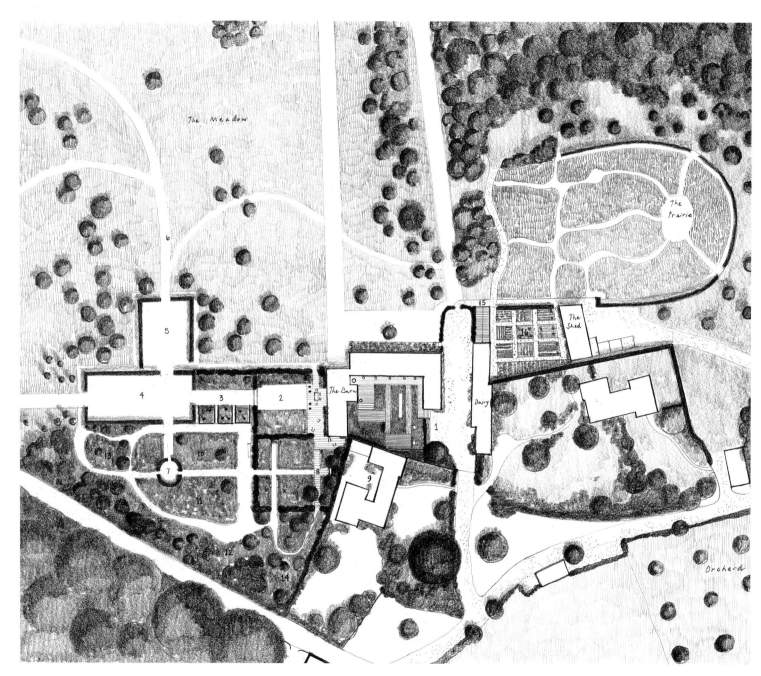

Plan of the Barn Garden, 2011. Serge Hill is immediately off the bottom of the plan. Drawn by Tom Stuart-Smith.

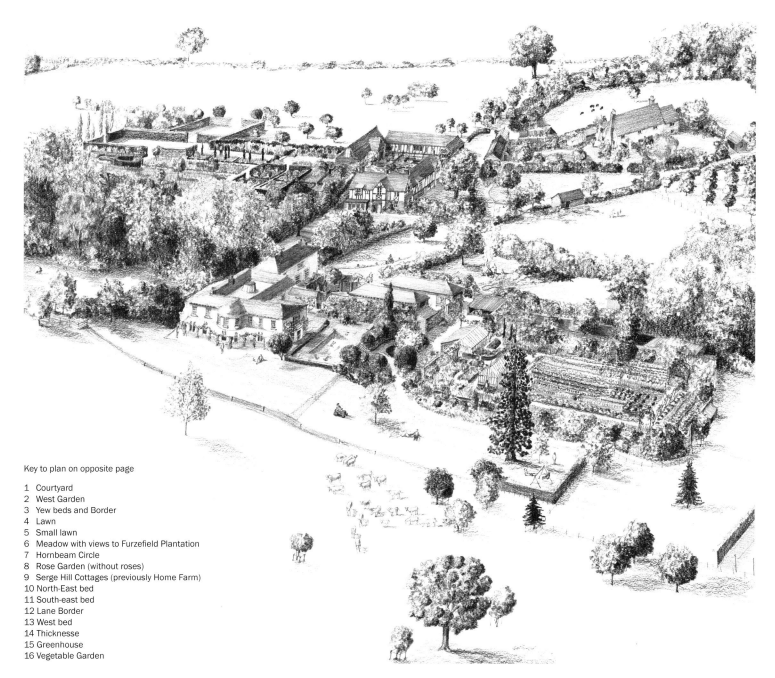

Key to plan on opposite page

1   Courtyard
2   West Garden
3   Yew beds and Border
4   Lawn
5   Small lawn
6   Meadow with views to Furzefield Plantation
7   Hornbeam Circle
8   Rose Garden (without roses)
9   Serge Hill Cottages (previously Home Farm)
10 North-East bed
11 South-east bed
12 Lane Border
13 West bed
14 Thicknesse
15 Greenhouse
16 Vegetable Garden

Aerial View of Serge Hill (detail), 2002. Drawn from memory as a present to Tom's parents for their golden wedding anniversary. The Barn and its garden are in the background with the Home Farm (as it was) between it and Serge Hill (foreground). Drawn by Tom Stuart-Smith.

Aerial photograph of Serge Hill Cottages (formerly the Home Farm) and the Barn c.1970

Making the Garden

Tom

For almost all of my life, home has been a corner of Hertfordshire at the centre of an equilateral triangle, with Watford, St Albans and Hemel Hempstead the defining coordinates. At night, the lights of the M1 and M25 encircle us like a bright necklace of sodium and in the hedge at the bottom of the garden you are as likely to encounter an abandoned fridge or cluster of empty beer cans as you are a foraging badger. But despite the noise and the dumping it remains a remarkable enclave of beauty, hanging by a thread.

My grandfather Tom Motion bought the Serge Hill estate in 1927 and married my granny in the same year. My mother was born here two years later and I was brought up here with my five brothers and sisters. It was an intensely fortunate, bucolic childhood and for long summer months blissfully isolated from the outside world. As a teenager I spent part of summer helping with the harvest on local farms, cleaning out grain silos, stacking bales of straw, walking home over the fields. For weeks at a time I worked in the woods with my father, thinning plantations, cutting firewood, planting trees, shooting squirrels.

Making a garden on the edge of this childhood territory has been the most engrossing project of my gardening life. Over nearly quarter of a century it has shaped my opinions about making gardens more than any other place. This is as much to do with learning from things I have got wrong as it has to do with my various successes. Making a garden for yourself is very different from doing it for somebody else. So much of the pleasure is to do with the coaxing and tending, the daily observance of small details and the accumulation of change over the years.

An Imaginary Garden

I began gardening for pleasure when I was about sixteen and my early experiments were much encouraged by my parents. After a degree in zoology at Cambridge I went to Manchester in 1982 to study landscape design but returned home as often as I could, bristling with plans for their garden. One of my more theoretical projects involved making a garden around some old farm buildings over the road from the house. These comprised a post-war milking shed, forlorn and rusting, a range of pig stys and a pretty 17th century timber framed barn, half full of mouldy straw and a moth-eaten collection of taxidermy. It was a magical, semi-abandoned place with the occasional cow making a home amongst the rusting seed drills.

I envisaged the farmyard transformed from a disparate mass of corrugated iron and orange baler twine into a serene assembly of platonic forms clipped out of box and yew that would float above a meadow-like sheet of flowers. I even made detailed plans and sketches for this improbable garden but had no expectation that we would ever do anything, or that anybody might live there.

Rebuilding the Barn

In 1986, Sue and I were married and later that year my parents offered us the same dilapidated barn as a home. They then proceeded to rebuild it, much of it with their own hands. My father had always built sheds, garages, huts and bridges and even three twenty-five foot ships complete with rudimentary cannons that were moored in woodland clearings, but the Barn was the first serious project. It actually had to stand up, keep the water out and see out more than just a decade or two. He and my mother took on a team of three bricklayers and two carpenters. All the sycamore and oak used on the floors was cut from the woods, seasoned and laid. Structural timbers were felled and hoisted into place the next day. There is one twelve foot high oak post in the north-west corner of the Barn which still has the bark on and I can recall exactly where this tree stood in Hanging Wood, some four hundred yards south of where it now holds up our roof.

So the house we live in emerged from the place and the people who live here; first in the seventeenth century when all the materials for its construction would have come from less than a mile away; timber from the surrounding woods or from previous buildings, flints, cobbles and lime from the fields. Then three hundred years later the process was repeated.

At fifty five feet long The Barn is not an especially grand construction but is has an ark-like presence. Forty pairs of twelve foot rafters hold up the roof, supported in turn by eight inch purlins and beams, every one different, so that the whole structure is startlingly asymmetrical. The west side seems to have sunk about a foot into the ground and the south gable leans in eighteen inches at the top. Outside, the eaves are two foot higher at one end than at the other. It looks as though it is gradually sinking into the ground. Which isn't, because the house sits on twenty foot of gravel.

Stones

The ground around the Barn from which these materials were extracted is a mishmash of recent geological origin. Deep underneath us lies the chalk which starts to form proper little hills about two miles to the north. On top of this is a muddle of gravel, hoggin and clay, all dumped by a vast glacier that came to a halt somewhere around here 400,000 years ago. The geology suggests that just to the south of us a great river was impounded by this glacial mess to form a lake, which finally burst its banks and moved further south to follow its present course, as the River Thames, through the centre of London. The glacier then retreated northward leaving its rubbish behind around the Barn. So it seems that this landscape was perhaps destined to be a dumping ground from the start.

The legacy of this geological fly tipping is all around us. My mother remembers before the Second World War, labourers picking up stones on the fields, paid by the bucket-full. Now, on the plough to the north of the house, by the end of winter, the surface is like a gravel drive and all that stone picking seems to have been a completely pointless labour.

When we came here I was obsessed by the stones and we spent a good proportion of the first two years raking barrowfulls off the ground. We regularly enlisted the help of family and friends in stone picking parties and tried to give the impression that this was the most desirable weekend activity imaginable. Tons of pebbles and flints were tipped under the blackthorn hedge on the north side of the garden. The farmyard was also full of compacted rubble, concrete and buried bits of indeterminate farm implement and the ubiquitous orange baler twine. If you tried to jam a fork in the ground, a jarring shock would run through your arm like electricity as you hit a ten inch flint.

There was an old, yellowing elder tree in the corner of the yard which was the only shrub or tree on the place. We hung on to it for about five years, getting increasingly bored of the little saplings popping up all over and replaced it with a walnut. On the other side of the Barn, in the space that was to become the main garden there was a monoculture of wheat stretching for fifty acres. We owned just a ten metre wide strip against the building and the farmer would spray pesticides up to the door. We felt like pioneers; twenty six years old, a baby and a view.

Joan and Murray (Tom's parents) at work in the garden, 1987. The central image shows Murray laying the stone edges in the Rose Garden. c.1991

Clockwise from top left: Tom and Sue with Rose in the coutyard 1988. Stonepicking 1990. The site of the future Prairie in 1990. Mid-summer feast in the field, 1991. Tom stone picking, 1990. Our friend the sculptor Martin Jennings hedge planting with Rose in pram, 1988.

Hedges

After several years of this, we got tired of the ploughed mud, the feeling that our children might be doused in fungicide and the lack of anywhere to roll about on the grass and we managed to buy five acres of the stony expanse. We started our gardening as a way of making sense out of the empty space that confronted us and made a series of compact domestic enclosures around the Barn. The hedge became our defining framework. To some extent this was a hangover from the arts and crafts gardens like Hidcote and Sissinghurst that I had visited with mother in my teens. I absorbed unquestioningly their language of sombre yew, shining beech and trim little box. I thought this is how gardens were made. But I also saw the structure of our plot as being a condensation of the surrounding pattern of Hertfordshire landscape into which our own patch was to be sown, like a bright square on a quilt.

The 1848 tithe map of St Stephen's parish, St Albans (p15) shows the Home Farm (as it was then called) surrounded by a patchwork of orchards, meadows and arable fields, generally between half an acre (closer to the farm) and ten acres. Within the seventy five acres surrounding the Barn there were, in 1848, sixteen separate fields and two woods. By 2008 this was reduced to two fields, three woods and a motorway. With the amalgamation of enclosures that began in the late nineteenth century much of the texture and history of the place has slipped away. A five acre field below the garden was named Botany Bay Meadow. What story did this contain? When the hedge was removed before the 1880's the name went with it and this, along with Upper Ninnings, Dead Woman's Field and Bloomy Croft were replaced by the blandness of North Field, an expanse of fifty acres which is as empty of resonance and connection as it is open and bleak.

The mixed hedges that remain in the landscape, full of hazel, holly, hornbeam and thorn become hedges of hornbeam and yew in the garden, and in some small way I feel that our hedgifying and gardening counteracts the gradual thinning out of detail in the wider landscape and lets us see afresh what is left. The spaces defined by our hedges become smaller and more intensely planted as one approaches the Barn and the outer curtilage of the garden is exactly defined so that nothing ornamental slips outside the green cage. The garden is delineated as just another compartment in the landscape.

Close to the Barn the hedges are all of yew, cut informally into bulbous mounds, which reflect the equally wonky nature of the Barn and the levels of the ground around it. On the more level area, forty metres west of the Barn, the hedges change to hornbeam. We keep them about ten foot tall and in contrast to the yew cut them as sharp as we can, defining the two empty rooms in the middle of the garden. Until recently I would cut these by standing on the roof of my father's pickup with a long armed hedge cutter while Sue drove very slowly and I tried not to fall off.

Garden and Landscape

At the same time as the hedge planting we put in many of the trees that surround the garden and sowed the meadow that borders the garden on two sides. It was a blackthorn summer in early April 1990 and with a party of friends we sowed the first acre broadcast by hand. The ground was clean after forty years of arable farming so we didn't have too much of weed problem. In the second year the meadow began to flower as a sheet of ox-eye daisies, improbably studded with blue spires of viper's bugloss. I was very proud of the daisies at the time but remember my bubble being burst by a grand cousin who on seeing our magnificent sheet of white remarked "ah yes.....motorway daisies". Five years on they had all but disappeared after this put-down and cowslips, scabious, birds foot trefoil, knapweed and buttercups became the more permanent residents

The garden is now made up of four semi enclosed spaces that are full of plants and two enclosed spaces that are empty green rooms. The composition of garden and Barn reads as one entity on the edge of the meadow and the outline has remained the same since the early 90's. The plan is arranged around two green axes that cross in the middle. The first begins at the west door of the Barn, runs through the larger of the green rooms in the middle of the garden, out into the meadow and ends in a ride cut through a wood about one hundred and fifty yards away. The cross axis begins in a small hornbeam hedged circle in the heart of the garden, surrounded by quite a large open area of herbaceous planting and crosses the other axis in the large green room, passes into a second empty room and ends in a view of meadow, sky and wood; so both forge a direct connection between an enclosed refuge and the landscape beyond.

As a child I used to have nightmares about wolves coming out of the wood at the bottom of the hill. Little could be more improbable, since Furzefield wood is a 1940's plantation. But it stretches to the horizon, steams with mist after a good summer rain and in my imagination I see it stretching, uninterrupted all the way to Scotland - not just to the Hemel-Hempstead road. The most fearsome occupants of this modern wildwood are not ferocious canines but burnt out cars and rusty washing machines, which add a home counties frisson to the concept of horizon as wilderness.

To the north there is no garden. The meadow comes up to the Barn so that you can be forgiven for thinking when you arrive at the house through the courtyard that you've seen the garden and the rest is just buttercups. I like the juxtaposition of the unkempt and the urbane – even if the latter can be a bit of a struggle. The different aspects of our temperament become reflected in the landscape that surrounds us, and there is a feeling of being in one type of space and seeing into another. There are moments here when you step out of the garden enclosure and are instantly in a landscape of wildflowers, hedgerows and broad horizons.

The enclosures close to the house are precisely defined, with areas of planting delineated in linear bands of old York stone. Some of these remain from the first beds I made with my father, who helped me build the early stages of the garden. There is a photograph of him standing in what was to be, for a ten year period, the rose garden, with its central path aligned on my old bedroom window at Serge Hill, something that occurred quite by chance. Today I look down the same path and can only just glimpse the big house though the oaks and hollies which have grown since the path was laid and I reflect that as I have reworked the content of the garden my father must sometimes have despaired at seeing so much of his work undone. But he has characteristically only rarely mentioned these depredations and then always more in jest at my profligacy and impatience for the next idea rather than in any tone of sustained injury. But the edgings in the rose garden remain - even if the roses have gone. In the photograph (p11) he stands, hands on hips, (a posture I have inherited) no doubt working out how to get around some thorny problem of pointing or bedding.

As you move further from the house the shape of the planting beds loosens up, the stone edges are dispensed with and the grass paths curve. The areas of planting become larger so that in the central area of the garden the beds are generally about six or seven metres wide. Some are double that. Because of this, plants are given a chance to dominate and there is a feeling, particularly in high summer, that as a visitor in the garden you are not so much incidental to the design as incidental to the growth and energy of plants.

In contrast to the courtyard garden, the main garden is very green. There is a small stone terrace close to the house but other than that almost everything is else is planted so that despite the plan of the garden being highly structured I think the effect is soft and natural.

The centre of the garden is empty. In the past I was tempted to fill this up with plants but the emptiness is needed in contrast to the density of the rest of it and gives the garden a calm, green, reflective heart.

Clockwise from top left: Sketch of the Home Farm and Barn courtyard 1837, found in the Portobello Road. The Tithe survey of St. Stephen's Parish, 1848, showing Serge Hill and the Home Farm with the surrounding fields and orchards. The Barn courtyard is apportionment no. 152; the barn in field 153 disappeared in the late 19th century. Drawings showing an idea for a garden in the Barn courtyard made as a student by Tom, 1984.

Clockwise from top left: Making hay, Tom planting in the field, Tom and Ben mulching, sowing the meadow with friends, loading hay with Rose, Ben and Harry. Sue sowing the meadow.
All between 1990-94

Clockwise from top left: The Barn in a wheat field 1988. Two views of daisies in the year after sowing the meadow, 1991. Rose in the Herb garden, 1991. The Rose garden in its first year, 1991. Wattle panels to protect planting in the west garden, 1991.

Following pages: Looking west from the Barn 2009. The arching grass is Stipa calamagrostis and the pink is Geranium "Patricia". The steps are made from granite road kerbs.

Previous pages: Tight hedges, loose hedges, fastigiate yew and herbaceous plants in the main garden west of the Barn. The tree is Sorbus sargentiana, 2009.

This page: clockwise from top left: The first courtyard garden, 2006, cutting it down, 2007, making the new garden from the pieces left over from Tom's garden for the Daily Telegraph at Chelsea 2006.

THE COURTYARD GARDEN

Sue

In January 2007, Tom and our youngest son Harry took a chainsaw to the hedges that formed the main structure of the Barn courtyard. I stood by and watched as twenty years of growth was toppled in less than twenty minutes.
It suddenly felt like an appalling act of vandalism. But once we started clearing away the debris, this feeling changed to one of liberation- a kind of garden revolution.

The courtyard at the Barn was the original farmyard and when we first arrived it was the only patch we were able to cultivate. Twenty years on, it was no longer a space we inhabited, it had become overgrown and the hedges were beset by box blight. We had been talking about how to change it for a number of years but could not settle on a plan.

Then in 2006, Tom made a Chelsea garden for The Daily Telegraph. I was captivated by the intense colours of the planting and the warm rust of the corten steel structures. At the end of the show it emerged that the rusty tanks and wall were unspoken for. They were due to be dismantled and transported to the contractor's yard with an uncertain future. Two things came together in my mind: the wish to preserve Tom's Chelsea garden and our need for change at home.
It seemed like a wonderful opportunity. Tom, in an end-of-show state of exhaustion, was unable to think about it but agreed that we would give a home to this mass of rusty steel. Within days of the show ending it arrived on a pantechnicon and was unloaded in our paddock. There it stayed for months on end with no clear plan emerging of how to install it within our own garden.

The challenge was about reworking the original design for the very different dimensions of our courtyard.
Months went by and the paddock started to resemble an overgrown scrap yard. We began to wonder if the idea was unworkable. Finally, in the New Year inspiration came and Tom drew up the plan. The original Chelsea team came down to the Barn to install the corten in its new home. The courtyard garden had previously been on three different levels.
The new design involved filling in the lowest level and meant importing a large amount of top soil. Moving the corten wall and tanks into the space involved heavy machinery as well as hair-raising moments because of their enormous weight and our restricted access.

The resulting transformation of the courtyard has been profound. The raising of the lower level gives a greatly increased sense of space. The tanks, which are filled with water, throw up light and cast reflections back into the house.
In summer, the courtyard becomes a living room that tempts even reluctant teenagers into the outside world.
The garden that had fallen into disuse is now at the centre of our daily lives.

The first courtyard garden, c. 2001. The Roses were Mary Rose and Gruss an Aachen. The central bed was planted with lettuce.

The first courtyard garden with box hedges, tulips and the elder tree, the only tree in the place when we arrived, c.1995.

Following pages: The courtyard garden in 2010 with Genista aetnensis in flower. In the foreground Euphorbia segueriana and Salvia nemerosa "Amethyst".

Previous pages: Reflections in the corten tank with Astrantia "Ruby Wedding" and Salvia nemorosa "Amethyst" in the courtyard garden.

This page: The vegetable garden in spring in 2010 with the old greenhouse. The tulips are left in after flowering.

THE VEGETABLE GARDEN

Sue

I am often asked whether there is part of the garden that is 'my patch', where I can do what I like. For the most part, the answer to that question is the vegetable garden which we created in 1998. Up until then we grew runner beans, cabbages & lettuces in the courtyard beds. But there are drawbacks to growing vegetables in amongst flowers, not least the gaping hole that your lunchtime lettuce leaves behind. Eventually the tension between edibility and aesthetics meant the vegetables needed a new home and we decided to create one with the idea that I would be its custodian.

We fenced off a small area adjoining the paddock using wattle fencing and planted a beech hedge inside it. The ground here was very poor and stony so we made four raised beds into which we imported some good soil and lots of manure. The layout centred on a hexagonal log cabin structure built by my father-in-law, Murray, when the children were small. It served as shelter for the donkeys and angorra goats that we kept in the paddock. Murray christened his structure the 'Domus Asinorum'. The name survived but in the new vegetable garden its occupants changed and it became a chicken house.

I took pride in cultivating this little patch and in summer, feeding our family from it. I experimented with oriental greens, patiently grew asparagus from seed and avoided pesticides as far as possible. At that stage we did not have a 'holding bed' and the veg/flower disputes would occasionally rear up again when Tom occupied a veg bed with plants that were destined for the main garden. Not that it was a flower free zone; we planted lots of multi-coloured tulips along the edges of the beds and they burst into exuberant colour in spring.

Although gardening is intrinsically about care and cultivation, it sometimes taps into a kind of territorial instinct, a wish to feel this is 'my domain' with a sense of being in control of what happens there. After we set up the vegetable garden we fell into the habit of spending weekends in our different domains, occasionally paying visits to find out what the other was up to. It was some years before we realised we were missing out on gardening together and we changed the way we garden. Making a garden brings both physical and emotional challenges. We have needed to sustain a sense of shared project whilst at the same time recognising that the Barn garden is Tom's creative vision.

In 2008 we decided to enclose the vegetable garden with a workshop on one side and a new greenhouse on the other. Ptolemy Dean designed a large tin structure for us and the building works were completed in 2010. As part of this change we doubled the area of the vegetable beds, so we have space to grow fruit and cutting flowers and at last there is room for a dispute-resolving 'holding bed'.

The vegetable garden, c.2007, with the "Domus Asinorum", by then already occupied by chickens.

Tulips in the Vegetable garden, including "Maureen", "Gavota", "Mickey Mouse", "Ballerina" and "Abu Hassan", with Ptolemy Dean's shed in the background, 2010.

Previous pages: 34 The meadow in spring with cowslips and pheasant eyes. 35 Euphorbia palustris and Narcissus "Thalia". Bamboo cloches used to protect plants from rabbits in spring.

This page: Eremurus "Joanna" and white Hesperis at the end of May.

PLANTING

Tom

In the first ten years or so I was learning about plants and wanting to experiment all the time. I kept piles of reference books and catalogues by our bed and was a totally irrepressible and irresponsible plant shopper. As a result, I changed the planting in the garden at an almost frenzied speed, with some plants making only brief cameo appearances before being cast onto the compost heap or being offered to friends. I recently looked through an old file of plant purchases dating from the late 80's through to the mid nineties and was a little shocked to see that perhaps only a quarter of any of the plants I bought during this period are now in the garden. Bergenias, Chrysanthemums, Cimicifugas, all gone.

The main criteria of our early plantings was that something had to be easy to propagate. I would buy five of a type from a nursery such as Beth Chatto or from Chris and Toby Marchant at Orchard Dene and then would meet my mother in her greenhouse over the road and strip them down into dozens of cuttings. Thousands of plants came out of her mist propagator and back over the road into our garden, including armfuls of Salvias, Penstemmons, Achilleas, Lilies, and Hellebores. We planted the garden a bed at a time, year by year, so the green container of hedges gradually began to fill.

Influence and Style

Like everyone I have been influenced by the changes in fashion and philosophy in the gardening world. I began by being inspired by two opposing traditions; the very English type of gardening exemplified by Sissinghurst and Hidcote and also by plant ecology. The garden that made the greatest impact on me during the 1980's was the Thijssepark in Amstelveen near Amsterdam, a miracle of naturalism created principally as an environmental educational project in the 1940's. The meeting and mixing of these two traditions continues at the Barn today.

Initially we went through quite a fluffy pink rose stage, clipped box, cranesbills and great swags of blousy pink Ispahan and purplish crimson Charles de Mills, worth growing for their names alone. But as the hedges and the roses grew, disease set in and I started to replace roses with more perennials. Eventually the roses in the Rose Garden were evicted entirely. This initial blousy pinkness overlapped with something of orange Kniphofia moment (which now seems a little improbable), then followed by a more wild Verbascum and opium poppy explosion in the early 90's and an increasingly grassy evolution over the last ten years as the pace of change has slowed.

Recently my planting has been influenced through friendship with Piet and Anja Oudolf and also by the wonderful Prairie planting created by Cassian Schmidt at Hermanshoff in Weinheim. I have tried to establish a planting character in the garden that evokes a natural diversity and abundance, something more redolent of a miraculous hedgebank than a grand display of horticultural wonders. In my attempt to establish this more naturalistic character I have gradually excluded the flagrantly exotic and cultivated. There is now not a single Kniphofia in the garden or an old fashioned rose or a delphinium. There are no polyanthus, pinks or double peonies. These are beautiful plants but I have decided, sometimes with real regret, that they don't have a place in the garden if we are to create a place where the character and mood is always more important than the collection of plants.

Supernormal gardening

I have increasingly come to see the planting in the garden like a cuckoo's egg that the song thrush is seduced into nurturing in preference to its own more modest offering; what the zoologists call a supernormal stimulus. Somewhere, half buried in the subconscious and in the interweaving clumps and drifts there is a connection to the hazel coppice and the verge thick with cow parsley and cranesbill, but the visual impact is more dramatic. I want the planting to evoke a sense of the confusingly semi-familiar, rather like the cuckoo's egg confuses the blackbird. It is both complex and varied but nothing is ever treated as a specimen. Plants have to muddle in and find their niche. So it is increasingly about creating a more sustainable vegetation that is diverse, beautiful and dramatic and less about growing any particular plant to perfection. The idea is not a bit new, although it has more to do with ecology than it does with conventional gardening. In line with this idea, plants in the garden are pretty well mixed up. There are no grand monocultural gestures, there being quite enough of those in the fields that surround us. In one place we have a patch of a beautiful small grass Hakonechloa that runs for about 8m along the base of the corten wall in the courtyard, but that's as designer-urban as we get.

A Gradient of Naturalism

Having said this, there are, close to the house a fair number of exotic and tender things: dahlias, penstemmons, the occasional sunflower or other annual and the odd climbing rose. But from here a gradient of naturalism rapidly kicks in so that as you walk further from the Barn all the plants are species or simple varieties and the colours become more locally connected. So out go the deep reds and rusts and in come the yellows, blues and purples, the colours of the meadow with the knapweed and trefoil. Towards the edges of the garden I also let wild plants creep into the mix, wild carrot, the occasional scabious, if it's a good one and foxgloves.

Throughout the garden, grasses make up about twenty five percent of all the planting. The percentage has increased gradually over the years as I have become more reliant on the structure and rhythm they give and their value in supporting other plants. Varieties of Miscanthus sinensis and Calamagrostis "Karl Foerster" are repeated through the garden and smaller Molinias, Stipas and Eragrostis make a textural connection with the grasses in the surrounding meadow. Grasses dilute the flower power of other perennials so the planting does not take on too artificial a character.

Tall Plants

The gravel has dictated what grows well and for the most part I fall in to line. Plants from hot and dry places such as sages, Stipas and Euphorbias are the most consistent and trouble free sorts but many of the things that give the height and form that I crave need extra help. At six foot five I wasn't really made to be an admirer of pebble sized saxifrages and have always loved plants that look me straight in the face, that give me the feeling of being amongst it all.

The battery of giants includes Maclaeya cordata, cardoon, species hollyhocks, Helianthus salicifolius and kellermanii which survive on nothing much, but for tall grasses, Veronicastrum, all the tall asters, Vernonias and a few others, our soil needs help. So while in most of the garden I leave the soil lean and mean for the Italians, Macedonians and Greeks, in other parts I plump it up for some of the more demanding Americans and Chinese.

In spring it is a race between Eremurus Joanna (a giant foxtail lily) which dominates the main west garden and Ferula communis (wild fennel). We have a dried flower of the Eremurus like a gargantuan pipe cleaner hanging in the Barn at a full thirteen foot, picked at the end of June as a vast, turgid, white spike. The dried remnant looks like a fossil from another

Cardoons, Hesperis and Eremurus at the end of May. Syringa x josiflexa "Bellicent" in the background.

Clockwise from top left: Asphedoline liburnica and Anthemis "Sauce Hollandaise", Eryngium giganteum, Cenolophium denudatum (both of which seed about), Cenolophium and Geranium "Rosenlicht", Salvia superba "Superba" and field scabious, more Asphedoline and Anthemis.

Following pages: Papaver orientale "Karine" with purple Salvia nemorosa "Ostfriesland" and an unamed yellow Verbascum.

era when things were bigger and more dangerous. Its descendents are slowly increasing in the garden and there are now about forty of them, swaying in the June breeze, a good four foot above anything else and quite a spectacle.The Fennel is as large but more fickle. It erupts into a frothy tumulus of leaf in late winter and then there is a short interlude of suspense when you wonder if it's going to do its thing. Then at a rate of up to four inches a day it launches its flower spike into the sky like an outrageous totem which then fans out into a canopy of golden flowers, perhaps the single most astonishing plant in the garden. It's all over shortly after midsummer leaving a gaping hole as a reminder of its previous splendour.

Inula racemosa forms giant virile clumps throughout the main part of the garden. In a wet summer the leaves are four foot long and a foot wide with spikes of rank yellow daisies topping out at about nine foot. In flower it is not elegant or pretty or an especially tasteful colour, but its got serious balls.

Delicacy

Of course it is good to throw the thugs into perspective by having a few diaphanous delicates around and through the large areas of planting there is a regular alternation between the brutes, the grasses and then more transparent things such as Thalictrum dipterocarpum. This is as insubstantial and tasteful as its possible to be, at seven foot, with a cloud of tiny mauve bells and dangling creamy anthers in August. The double flowered variety "Hewitts double" flowers a little later and longer but lacks the microscopic elegance of the single. Thalictrum "Elin" closer to the house is even larger, ten foot in good soil and a pale cream blur over glaucous leaves, wonderful when set against the leaning, towering weight of Eupatorium purpureum "Riesenschirm".

At a smaller scale, the Carthusian pink, Dianthus carthusianorum comes as a surprise for those used to old fashioned pinks. The bright cerise flowers, half an inch across are held up to three foot by such thin stems that they seem to float disembodied from any support. I mix it up with Salvias, sedums, Acnatherum calamagrostis and low asters in the walk from the rose garden to the hornbeam circle. It seems to flower for ever (which means June to August). Cephleria dipsacoides operates at a higher level, perhaps five foot. It doesn't give you quite the same flower power as the more commonly grown Cepheria gigantea, but it is much more drought tolerant and has the same tone of delicate creamy flowers but above a resilient architecture of wiry stems that it cousin lacks. All these airy plants do more than any others to give a garden a diaphanous naturalism that comes both from seeing things through other things and by creating movement, without them planting can easily become what our daughter Rose used to called "bunchy".

One of the contradictory effects of using large plants is to make the garden feel bigger. It's the same effect that furnishing a room has and comes about from the greater subdivision of space. Consequently, as the garden becomes more overgrown in summer it also seems to expand gently before retracting again in winter. Sentinels seem to accentuate this effect of increased spaciousness. The spires of verbascums and hollyhocks become like the spires of the city churches in early eighteenth century views of London, where it seems that the city goes on for ever.

Many of these sentinels are biennial: Verbascums, Peucedenums or Onopordum are all bolt upright and give a little rigor to an ensemble that might otherwise become a bit too whimsy and floaty. I remember bringing an American friend around the garden one summer when I had let the population of seven foot mulleins and scotch thistles get a little out of control. " Tom... your garden is so aggressive!" she cried.

Previous pages: 44-45 Late spring in the Rose Garden with orange Euphorbia griffithii "Dixter", pale blue Amsonia hubrichtii, cerise Geranium psilostemmon, Allium "Purple Sensation" and spikes of Eremurus "Cleopatra". 46-47 Looking over the Rose Garden in July with tall Maclaeya cordata, cerise Geranium psilostemmon, rust red Helenium "Moorheim Beauty", Bronze Fennel and Salvia sclarea "Turkestanica"

This page: Winter views in the main garden. Clockwise from top left: Looking towards the Rose garden, Inula racemosa and Miscanthus, three views of the yew beds with low clipped box. The two main garden axes to the north and to the west. The yew beds looking towards the Barn.

Many of these plants need space between them to be at their most effective, and those that require baking in the sun, the stipas, giant fennels, and Eremurus would just shrink and eventually disappear if not given a bit of elbow room. I have therefore tended to fill the spaces between the tall plants with lower, more gentle moundy things like phloxes, astrantias, geraniums and amsonias. Every star needs its understudy, plants that are happy to weave in and out or can thrive in a bit of shade.

Leaves

Texture and form is much more important to me in the planting than is flower colour, and the form of the flower and its size is also something I think about as much as the subtlety of tone. All of the plantings at the Barn contain repeated clumps of strongly structured plants that hold the whole matrix together. Grasses are the most important in that they stand up well and give glossy, strappy or feathery contrast to all the rest from May to October. Other plants can also be used to give repeated structure, but all must have the virtue of retaining strong form even when out of flower. So I use things with some real backbone and distinctive foliage like Euphorbia, Eupatorium, Veronicastrum and Silphium in repeated groups to give some bold rhythm and simplicity to the planting, between which a more complex collection of stuff can weave.

As the garden has developed I have concentrated more on how the garden looks out of the peak season. Asters, Echinaceas, Sanguisorbas, and late salvias all look perfectly decent though the summer but don't collapse into a messy heap in September like someone leaving a party at ten o'clock. I also use more plants now that are quite subtle in flower but always look elegant. Amsonias, which work well on this soil are chief amongst these and I am yet to find one that isn't worth growing, Euphorbia, Sedum, Epimedium come into the same category.

Winter

Grasses have great presence in winter, more solid than anything offered by other perennial plants. The best, such as Miscanthus sinensis "Malepartus" combine grace and indestructibility. Then there is Calamagrostis "Karl Foerster" with a tight bunch of stick-vertical straws, all very architectural at five foot. Panicums generally have a bit more colour and stand up quite well, and the giant oat grass, Stipa gigantea is a virtually everlasting seven foot diaphanous starbust. My favourite dead grass in January is the comparatively diminutive Hakonechloa macra, which in its plain un-variegated form in the courtyard and rose garden looks like a slightly exotic version of something you might find at the base of an old hedge in Dorset; glossy, tufty and arching gracefully. It is one of the few grasses to keep some warm colouring into the New Year.

The garden is not planted for winter flower or colour. There is no extravaganza of red and yellow stems, very few berries, no variegation and no spikey phormiums or yuccas to liven things up into a state of subtropical delusion. This may sound perversely gloomy but I have always wanted the garden in winter to look like it is in the full grip of the cold and not in a state of seasonal denial. Of the taller plants, Veronicastrums, Aster Novae-Angliae and Inula magnifica are amongst the most rigid and the darkest to die, Rudbeckias are also excellent for dark shapes and blackish seedheads, but tend to struggle on our soil. Rich browns are especially useful to dispel the overall dreariness, so I value Vernonia crinita, like a seven foot large leaved aster, which keeps its seed heads and the stems remain a deep foxy brown- very handsome with bleached Miscanthus. Also at a lower level sedums are superb for rich browns, especially the pewter leaved "Matrona" and smaller, purpler "Karl Funkelstein".

Winter in the courtyard with the grass, Hakonechloa macra against the corten wall. Furniture by Paola Lenti.

Frozen tanks and Hakonechloa.

Following pages: 52 Inula recemosa and Miscanthus sinensis "Kleine Silberspinne"; 53 Cardoons and Miscanthus sinensis "Malepartus"; 54-55 Hoar frost in the main garden. Left, the hornbeam circle. Right, Stipa gigantea.

Previous pages: Looking north from the Barn in winter to the plantation with the Bodger's Hovel built in the meadow by Ben and Harry, 2010.

This page: The garden in the mid to late 90's with the Rose Garden, Turkish tent and early perennial plantings. The tent, which had a wooden roof, came from a Chelsea Flower Show garden made with Elizabeth Banks in 1992. We took it down every winter and hung the curtains in the Barn.

Cutting back

We start the cutting back over the Christmas holidays. A few years ago I wandered out into the garden after a rather heavy Christmas lunch to see that half the grasses in one part of the garden seems to be tilting at about ten degrees off the vertical. For a moment I wondered if it was me that was falling over, but closer inspection revealed that about thirty clumps of Molinia, Panicum and Hakonechloa had been hollowed out by mice underneath so that there was just a thin helmet of root left with the foliage attached. Rolo, our Dachshund was clearly spending too much time curled up in front of the fire. I quickly cut back the other grasses and plants and the problem stopped. I suspect the two barn owls that roost in our garage had a mid winter feast now that the cover was consigned to the compost heap.

Spring

In spring when the perennial planting is quiet, there is an early blooming of Magnolias and Malus, but the main event is the succession of bulbs, beginning with snowdrops in February and continuing through Scillas , Chinodoxas, white and pale yellow narcissi, to the later tulips and the incomparable Narcissus poeticus recurvus which we have planted by the thousand. Getting the smaller bulbs to have an impact over an acre of garden takes time. Ten years of determined snowdrop and Scilla planting its now just beginning to tell, with small clumps coalescing to form little swathes, even drifts. In another ten years I hope that the garden will pulse from the white of snowdrops to the blue of Scillas, Anenomes and Chinodoxas before the white narcissi and golden heads of Euphorbia palustris light up the whole place in April.

At this time of year we do quite a bit of staking, with Hazel if there is enough about. We go to quite a bit of trouble making moundy cat's cradles for the plants that would otherwise topple over, including most tall Thalictrums, Sanguisorbas and even Veronicastrums. These are plants that stand up on more moisture retentive soils, but here, if we get a dry period in high summer, they collapse.

The Courtyard Planting

In its previous life at the Chelsea Flower Show I had designed a garden as an expression of the meeting of the modern and the romantic. Modernism is so often connected with minimalism in garden design, with planting being reduced to monocultures or tasteful combinations of "plant material" that complement rather than contrast. I wanted to make a garden that was all about contrast, between a garden plan that was so simple it was almost mundane, and a content that was full of texture, detail and colour. This opposition remains in its reincarnated state at the Barn. The plan is simple and linear but the planting is very colourful and complex. The corten is a resolutely modern material, but it also recalls the rusty past of the farmyard.

The planting in the courtyard is the most colourful in the garden and takes its lead from the brown of the steel and the orange clay roof tiles. Some of the plants are the same as those I used in the Chelsea garden. These include richly coloured bearded Irises "Attention please", "Supreme Sultan", "Provencal", "Vintage Wine", and other perennials such as Astrantia "Ruby Wedding", Euphorbia grifithii "Dixter", Salvia "Ostfriesland", Sedum Matrona, and the grasses Hakonechloa macra and Anemanthele lessoniana.

But the planting needed to be more balanced over the seasons than in the Chelsea original. In spring most of the colour comes from bulbs. Snowdrops such as "Sam Arnott" and "Mighty Atom" are succeeded by dwarf narcissi and scillas, but the first big event is the tulip.

Tulips and Euphorbia x martinii in the courtyard. Tulip "Couleur Cardinal" bottom right.

Tulips and brown foliage of Carex testacea. Tulip "Abu Hassan" far right with a golden edge to the flower.

Following pages: Astrantia "Ruby Wedding", Iris "Supreme Sultan" and Stipa gigantea in the courtyard.

Previous pages: The courtyard in July. Left: Salvia nemorosa "Amethyst", Salvia nemorosa "Ostfriesland", Genista aetnensis.
Right: Euphorbia segueriana and Stipa gigantea in the courtyard

This page: Making the Prairie, winter 2010-2011
Top right and bottom left, Tom's design studio put to work

We use a range of bright colours and striped tulips. It changes every year but Abu Hassan, Paul Scherer, Havran, Curly Sue, Mickey Mouse, Ballerina, Helmar, Jan Reus, Princess Irene, Zurel are all regular visitors. They contrast well with the early flowers of Euphorbia x martini and the rusty steel. Following this the bearded Irises get into their swing, soon followed by Salvias and Astrantias. But the high point of summer undoubtedly comes in early July with the flowering of the brooms, which is accompanied by Euphorbia segueriana, various eryngiums and Ratibida pinnata, the Mexican hat, whose little, acid yellow flowers with black cones, float about in the wind above a lot of Panicum grass. In late summer Echinacea purpurea "Magnus", various vinous sedums and origanums combine to make a strong purple front which contrasts with yellows and russets, including Coreopsis verticillata and Achillea "Walter Funke". The intention is that throughout the year the planting creates the effect of a more or less random tapestry that does not appear too composed.

Only a few of the climbers and the large plant of Leptospermum lanigerum remain from the earlier garden.
The broom which provides the vertical structure without the shade is Genista aetnensis and will grow to about twenty five feet in time, throwing a delicate shade over the whole courtyard. With the exception of an Osmanthus hedge around the garden and a few euphorbias, the planting is entirely herbaceous.

The Meadow

The meadow is the key to the garden setting. In spring there are a lot of cowslips, quite surprising considering our dry gravelly soil, then narcissi, native and pheasant eyes. The other good moment is at the end of June into July when the knapweeds, scabious, trefoil, yarrow and field cranesbill start up and the colours of the flowers inside the garden tend to reflect the purples, blues and yellows in the field. In 2010 we sowed a number of other little meadows close by, in the hope that over time we can create more of a wildflower and butterfly network around the Barn.

In and around the meadow and garden we have planted several hundred trees. Most of them native and those that aren't have a fairly low-key subtlety about them. Around the garden the trees have to be drought tolerant and we have planted mainly holm oak, species malus, Zelkova, chestnut, cockspur thorn, lime, ash and above all oak.
Oak is the defining tree of this landscape, both in and out of the garden.

The Prairie

In January 2011 we seeded half an acre of ground to the east of the garden with a mix of mainly North-American perennials to make an exotic meadow. I have worked on a number of projects over the last eight years with Professor James Hitchmough at Sheffield University who has developed the techniques of seeding exotic perennials as a means of creating colourful vegetation that can be established and maintained for a fraction of the cost of conventional planting. This is for a number of reasons: The density of plants is much higher, perhaps a hundred per square metre, so there is less room for weeds in the first place, the seeding is done through a three inch layer of sand which acts as a weed suppressant and nothing is done to improve the soil, so there are fewer nutrients for weeds to get exited about. The other distinct characteristic of this type of vegetation is that it is very attractive in the latter part of the year, climaxing in August when, even with the best intentions, the main part of the garden can look a bit tired.

In the first years the planting will be dominated by Rudbeckias, Echinaceas and Asters but as time goes on tall Silphiums will give it a more interesting and multilayed character and various shrubs such as Cotinus, Sassafras, Aronia and Rhus will be added to give it some bulk.

The Prairie is divided by grass paths sown with grasses which won't migrate into the exotic areas. One part of the field is over clay and the other part on gravel so there are different seed mixes for each area. Periodically we might need to burn the garden in late winter to destroy weeds and slugs. Supposedly, all the prairie plants are entirely resistant to this sort of treatment having been subjected to it over several hundred millennia.

A Broader View

In recent years I have come to see the garden less as a series of events and more as part of a place in a landscape, an intermediary between the barn and its wider setting. With the disappearance of the rose garden and herb garden, the detail and character of the place and its planting has therefore become more part of an narrative of atmosphere and less a series of vignettes. Within the hedged enclosure, the planting is like a gradually changing stream of vegetation that flows through the architecture of the garden.

At the same time, our gardening has become as much to do with nurturing a patch of vegetation as is to do with growing individual plants. There is much more repetition than there used to be and no sudden transformations of character, so that the quality of planting at one end of the garden is different from that at the other but there are no hard lines or sudden changes and there are even moments when there is a unifying sweep of effect through the whole place.

Over the last few years I have also freed up the structure, opening views diagonally across the grain and making visual connections that enable the eye, if not always the feet, to follow a drift of planting across the garden.
This has given a stronger counterpoint between the axial vistas that slice through the garden and the more open sweeps that take in panoramas of planting, so there is often a difference between the path you walk and the place you look.
For example, after ten years the first yew hedge that we had planted around the Barn to separate us from the field to the west had grown to seven foot and we were being confined to a box with one main view out. While this hedge had been growing we had planted up the field on the far side but now couldn't see it. In a burst of chainsaw enthusiasm I cut the hedge in half. It was one of the more creative acts of destruction I have perpetrated on the garden. For a year or so it was raw, but now the dark wall is transformed into a satisfyingly bloated worm over which there is a suggestion of something interesting and a little remote. Our view out is no longer confined to a single allee down the centre, but roves over a broader sweep.

As the garden has grown, the structural framework of hedges, openings, diagonal vistas, crowded, planty spaces and empty, green rooms has taken on an increasingly strong presence in my mind as a kind of virtual garden where I spend perhaps even more time wandering in than I do in the real one. And I reflect that the garden at the Barn began like this, as an imagined place, before it ever became a reality. The architecture and the content of the real garden spaces has become a frame through which I see the outside world. There seems to be a similarity between the enfilades and enclosures of the garden and the opportunities and territories of my own imaginative life and that of my family. The edges of the garden have become like the meeting point between inner and outer reality, between the mind and the world.

Previous page: view over west garden in early summer with Nepeta "Walker Low" in the foreground and the spires of Eremurus "Joanna" beyond.
This page: Crataegus x lavallei in the Meadow

The Meadow in July

Following pages: 72-73 The Barn from the north
74-75 The Meadow in late summer

Previous pages: The Meadow in July

This page clockwise from top left: Wooden recliner in the hornbeam enclosure. Harry scoring a goal. Sue with Rolo. The hammockry. Camping in the Meadow.

Garden and Growth

Sue

      I wrote this in 2004. There were very few trees here when we started and in the early years Tom planted hundreds, often with a baby strapped to his back. In hot summers we longed for shade. Then finally in 2003, the trees in our secluded grove of Zelkovas, Sweet Chestnuts and Ilex had grown large enough for us to create a hammockry.

      The garden represents a kind of timeline in our lives.
It has grown and changed alongside the growing up of children and family.
It started out with stone picking the fields,
hand sowing the meadow and planting embryonic hedges and trees.

      In the beginning it was an idea of a garden and over time it has formed a place
with a unique sense of being, like a baby becoming a person.
While you look away from it, it silently gets on with growing
and then surprises you when on looking back you see how far it has come on.
The trees that were once saplings are suddenly strong enough to hold a hammock
and create a place within the place to retreat to.

      The garden is peopled by memories as well as by plants:
The water fights, the Easter egg hunts,
the long summer lunches, the games of partridges.
Layers of memory are grafted onto the place in our minds.

      Just as memories are a resource, so the garden is a resource.
It is a repository of beauty – something to turn to when tired and empty.
It gives back much more than it takes.

Hornbeam hedges in the west garden, looking north.

Hornbeam hedges looking west.

Following pages: 80-81 View from a hot air balloon, 2010. Serge Hill is just visible top left.

The Plants

This is a rough list of the plants in the garden at the beginning of 2011. It doesn't include many bulbs or anything recently planted or present in too small an amount to be significant. For location see plan on page 6.

The Sheds and Courtyard Garden
Shrubs and Climbers

Ceanothus "Concha"
Clematis "Etoile Violette"
Clematis "Royal Velours"
Clematis alpina "Frances Rivis"
Clematis armandii "Apple Blossom"
Clematis orientalis "Bill McKenzie"
Daphne bholua "Jaqueline Postill"
Eupatorium ligustrinum
Euphorbia mellifera
Euphorbia x pasteurii
Genista aetnensis
Hedera helix "Pedata"
Itea ilicifolia
Juglans regia
Laurus nobilis "Angustifolia"
Leptospermum lanigerum
Osmanthus heterophyllus
Parthenocissus henryana
Phlomis italica
Pileostegia viburnoides
Rosa chinensis "Sanguinea"
Rose "Alberic Barbier"
Rose "Etoile de Hollande"
Schizophragma integrifolia
Shizandra grandiflora "Rubriflora"
Vitis vinifera "Purpurea"

Herbaceous

Achillea "Walter Funke"
Astrantia major "Ruby Wedding"
Coreopsis verticillata "Zagreb"
Digitalis ferruginea
Echinacea purpurea "Magnus"
Eryngium bourgatii forms
Euphorbia cornigera
Euphorbia segueriana niciciana
Euphorbia x martinii
Hakonechloa macra
Helleborus orientalis forms
Iris Tall Bearded "Provencal"
Iris Tall Bearded "Attention Please"
Iris Tall Bearded "Superstition"
Iris Tall Bearded "War Sails"
Origanum "Rosenkuppel"
Panicum virgatum "Shenandoah"
Pulmonaria "Blausmeer"
Ratibida pinnata
Salvia nemorosa "Amethyst"
Salvia nemorosa "Ostfriesland"
Sedum "Karl Funkelstein"
Sedum "Matrona"
Sporobolus heterolepsis
Stipa arundinacea
Stipa calamagrostis

West Garden
Shrubs and Climbers

Abutilon x suntense
Clematis alpina "Frances Rivis"

Euphorbia stygiana
Euphorbia characias subsp. wulfenii
Hydrangea quercifolia
Lonicera periclymenum "Graham Thomas"
Penstemmon "Raven"
Phillyrea latifolia
Phlomis italica
Phygelius "Moonraker"
Rosa "Sombreuil"
Rosa chinensis "Mutabilis"
Rose "Alister Stella Gray"
Solanum x crispum "Glasnevin"
Syringa microphyla "Superba"
Viburnum x carlesii "Aurora"
Wisteria sinensis

Herbaceous

Althea "Parkallee"
Aster laevis "Arcturus"
Aster novae-angliae "Lou Williams"
Calamintha nepeta
Cynara cardunculus
Epilobium angustifolium "Stahl Rose"
Eryngium giganteum
Eupatorium maculatum "Orchard Dene"
Eupatorium maculatum "Reisenschirm"
Eupatorium rugosum "Chocolate"
Geranium "Patricia"
Geranium "Sue Crug"
Geranium "Rozanne"
Geranium psilostemmon
Hakonechloa macra
Helleborus x ericsmithii
Helleborus orientalis forms
Maclaeya cordata
Miscanthus sinensis "Ferne Osten"
Miscanthus sinensis "Malepartus"
Nepeta "Walker's Low"
Origanum "Rosenkuppel"
Phlox paniculata "Lavendelvolke"
Romneya coulteri
Sedum "Matrona"
Selinum wallichianum
Stipa calamagrostis
Teucrium hycanicum
Thalictrum "Elin"
Thalictrum dipterocarpum "Album"
Verbascum "Spica"
Verbascum "Polarsomer"
Verbascum lychnitis
Veronicastrum virginicum "Fascination"

Yew border
Shrubs

Buddleia "Dartmoor"
Eleagnus commutata "Quicksilver"

Herbaceous

Achillea "Coronation Gold"
Achillea "Gold Plate"
Anthericum lilago

Amsonia tabernaemontana var. salicifolia
Anthemis tinctoria "Susannah Mitchell"
Aster turbinellus
Cynara cardunculus
Epilobium angustifolium "Album"
Euphorbia segueriana niciciana
Helianthus "Lemon Queen"
Knautia macedonica
Miscanthus sinensis "Malepartus"
Nepeta nuda
Panicum "Cloud Nine"
Salvia guaranitica
Salvia nemorosa "Mainacht"
Salvia pratensis "Indigo"
Salvia x superba "Superba"
Stachys byzantina "Big Ears"
Stipa brachytricha
Thalictrum flavum glaucum

Yew beds

Allium christophii
Allium spaerocephalon
Amsonia tabernaemontana var salicifolia
Anthemis "Sauce Hollandaise"
Asphedoline liburnica
Crambe maritima
Erisymium "Bowles' Mauve"
Eryngium bourgatii forms
Euphorbia cyparasius "Fenn's Ruby"
Geranium "Phillippe Vapelle"
Geranium himalayense
Geranium sanguineum
Nepeta x faassenii
Ruta graveolens "Jackman's Blue"
Salvia blancoana
Salvia officinalis "Purpurascens"
Salvia argentea
Scabiosa lucida
Taxus baccata "Fastigiata"

Rose Garden
Shrubs and Climbers

Cotinus obovatus
Ligustrum lucidum
Maytenus boaria
Viburnum x hillieri "Winton"
Wisteria sinensis

Herbaceous

Achillea "Gold Plate"
Achillea "Walter Funke"
Aconitum "Stainless Steel"
Allium christophii
Amsonia hubrichtii
Amsonia orientalis
Aster "Little Carlow"
Aster novae-angliae "Marina Wolkonsky"
Aster novae-angliae "Violetta"
Astrantia major "Ruby Wedding"
Atriplex hortensis "rubra"
Campanula lactiflora

Dahlia "Dark Desire"
Dahlia "Ragged Robin"
Echinacea purpurea "Magnus"
Echinops ritro "Veitch's Blue"
Epimedium "Frohnleiten"
Eremurus "Cleopatra"
Eryngium agavefolium
Euphorbia grifithii "Dixter"
Foeniculum vulgare "Giant Bronze"
Geranium pratense "Plenum Violaceum"
Geranium psilostemmon
Hakonechloa macra
Helenium "Moorheim Beauty"
Helenium "Rubinsverg"
Hemerocallis "Black Plush"
Knautia macedonica
Maclaeya cordata
Miscanthus sinensis "Gracillimus"
Miscanthus sinensis "Silberfeder"
Panicum virgatum "Rehbraun"
Pennisetum alopecuroides "Hameln"
Phlox paniculata "Blue Paradise"
Rudbeckia fulgida var sullivanii "Goldsturm"
Salvia sclarea "Turkestanica"
Sanguisorba officinalis "Tanna"
Sedum "Karl Funkelstein"
Sedum "Morchen"
Silphium perfoliatum
Silphium terebinthinaceum
Thalictrum aquilegifolium
Thalictrum dipterocarpum
Vernonia crinita "Mammuth"

Big Bed NE

Aconitum "Spaetlese"
Agastache "Blue Fortune"
Amsonia tabernaemontana var salicifolia
Aquilegia alpina
Aralia racemosa
Aster macrophyllus "Twilight"
Aster umbellatus
Buglosoides purpocaerulea
Calamagrostis acutiflora "Karl Foerster"
Campanula lactiflora
Cephlaria alpina
Cephlaria dipsacoides
Cirsium rivulare "Atropurpureum"
Dianthus carthusianorum
Digitalis grandiflora
Eragrostis curvula
Eremurus "Joanna"
Euphorbia palustris
Geranium "Patricia"
Geranium phaeum
Geranium psilostemmon
Gillenia trifoliata
Hesperis matrionalis
Inula racemosa "Sonnenspeer"
Knautia macedonica
Magnolia cylindrica
Miscanthus sinensis "Graziella"
Miscanthus sinensis "Kleine siberspinne"
Perovskia atriplicifolia "Blue Spire"

Phlomis anatolica "Lloyds variety"
Phlomis russeliana
Phlox "Violetta Gloriosa"
Salvia nemorosa "Blauhugel"
Salvia pratensis "Indigo"
Salvia uliginosa
Salvia x superba "Superba"
Sanguisorba officinalis "Arnhem"
Scabiosa columbaria
Sedum "Matrona"
Sorbus sargentiana
Stipa arundinacea
Stipa brachytricha
Stipa gigantea
Thalictrum dipterocarpum "Hewitts Double"
Thalictrum flavum
Verbascum unknown
Veronicastrum "Lavendelturm"

Big Bed SE

Agastache "Blue Fortune"
Althea rugosa
Amsonia hubrichtii "Ernst Pagels"
Amsonia tabernaemontana var salicifolia
Anemone x hybrida "Queen Charlotte"
Astrantia major "Alba"
Campanula persicifolia
Campanula rotundifolia
Cenolophium denudatum
Dianthus carthusianorum
Euphorbia palustris
Euphorbia seravschanica
Geranium "Nimbus"
Geranium sylvaticum "Mayflower"
Inula magnifica "Sonnenstrahl"
Inula racemosa
Iris siberica "Persimmon"
Miscanthus sinensis "Gracillimus"
Miscanthus sinensis "Yakushima dwarf"
Molinia caerulea "Strallenqulle"
Molinia caerulea var arundinacea "Transpa-rent"
Nepeta nuda
Panicum virgatum"Shenandoah"
Persicaria amplexicaule "Rosea"
Persicaria amplexicuale "Taurus"
Persicaria polymorphum
Phlox paniculata Mt. Fujiyama
Phytolacca americana
Salvia nemorosa "Carradona"
Sanguisorba officinalis "Cangshan Cranberry"
Stipa brachytricha
Strobilanthes atropurpurea
Veronicastrum virginicum "Fascination"
Veronicastrum virginicum "Spring Dew"

Lane Border
Trees and Shrubs

Magnolia x Proctoriana
Zelkova verschaffeltii
Prunus lusitanica "Myrtifolia"
Magnolia loebneri "Merrill"
Viburnum rhytidophyllum
Osmanthus heterophyllus
Osmanthus burkwoodii
Syringa x Prestoniae vars
Rosa pimpinellifolia Double White

Rose "Pauls Himlayan Musk"
Amelanchier canadensis
Magnolia x loebneri "Leonard Messel"
Phillyrea angustifolia var. rosmarinifolia

Herbaceous

Acanthus mollis
Aconitum arendsii "Kelmscott"
Anemone x hybrida "Queen Charlotte"
Cardamine pentaphyllos
Chaerophyllum hirsuitum
Epimedium rubrum
Epimedium versicolor "Sulphureum"
Eupatorium maculatum album
Galega orientalis
Geranium "Rosenlicht"
Geranium Brookside
Geranium nodosum
Geranium phaeum album
Helleborus oreintalis
Lunaria rediviva
Molinia caerulea Heidebraut
Paeonia "Late Windflower"
Phlox divuricata "Blue Perfume"
Polemonium vars
Smilacina racemosa
Thermopsis montana

West End
Trees and Shrubs

Aesculus pavia "Atrosanguinea"
Daphne tanguitica
Magnolia stellata
Philadelphus "Belle Etoile"
Quercus phellos
Rosa canina "Abbotswood"
Sorbus aria "Magnifica"
Syringa pekinensis
Viburnum tinus "Gwenlian"

Herbaceous

Aster "Anja's Choice"
Aster umbellatus
Calamagrostis acutiflora "Karl Foerster"
Cenolophium denudatum
Ferula communis
Paeonia "Jan van Leeuwen"
Papaver orientale "Karine"
Papaver orientale "Pattys Plum"
Persicaria amplexicaule "Alba"
Phlomis russeliana
Salvia "Lapis Lazuli"
Salvia nemorosa "Amethyst"
Thermopsis sp

Thicknesse
Trees and Shrubs

Corylopsis spicata
Camellia sasanqua
Prunus "Accolade"
Choisya ternata
Sambucus nigra "Laciniata"
Camellia x williamsii "St Ewe"
Osmanthus heterophyllus

Rosa californica "Plena"
Rosa virginiana

Herbaceous

Asarum europaeum
Datisca cannabiana
Epimediums (various)
Eupatorium maculatum "Purpureum"
Euphorbia "Whistleberry Garnet"
Euphorbia cornigera
Euphorbia x pasteurii
Inula magnifica
Maclaeya cordata
Melopospermum peloponnesiacum
Paeonia mlokosewitschii
Phlox paniculata "Hesperis"
Pulmonaria "Blausmeer"
Pulmonaria "Blue Ensign"
Pulmonaria "Sissinghurst White"
Rodgersia pinnata "Superba"
Selinum wallichianum
Symphytum "Hidcote Blue"
Thalictrum lucidum

Prairie
sown January 2011 with a seed mix devised
by James Hitchmough

clay soil

Amorpha canescens
Andropogon gerardii
Aster azureus
Aster novae-angliae 'Septemberubrin'
Aster oblongifolius
Aster turbinellus
Baptisia pendula
Carex testacea
Coreopsis tripteris
Echinacea pallida
Echinacea purpurea 'Prairie Splendour'
Eryngium yuccifolium
Galtonia candicans
Lobelia tupa
Rudbeckia fulgida var deamii
Rudbeckia maxima
Silene regia
Silphlum terebinthlnaceum
Silphum laciniatum
Solidago speciosa
Sorghastrum nutans
Hesperantha coccinea pink forms
Kniphofia uvaria (Eastern Cape Form)
Melanthium virginicum
Moraea spathulata

sandier soil

Amorpha canescens
Andropogon gerardii
Asclepias tuberosa
Aster azureus
Aster oblongifolius
Callirhoe bushii
Carex testacea
Dianthus carthusianorum
Dracocephalum rupestre
Echinacea pallida

Echinacea paradoxa
Echinacea purpurea 'Prairie Splendour'
Echinacea tenessenssis Rocky Top hybrids
Eryngium yuccifolium
Euphorbia corollata
Galtonia candicans
Kniphofia triangularis Liatris aspera
Liatris scariosa 'Alba'Lobelia tupa
Oenothera macrocarpa var incana
Penstemon barbatus Coccineus
Penstemon cobaea
Scutellaria baicalensis
Silene regia
Silphium laciniatum
Silphium terebinthinaceum
Solidago speciosa
Castilleja integra
Gentiana andrewsii
Gladiolus papilio ex Ruby
Moraea spathulata
Kniphofia uvaria (Eastern Cape Form)

Trees
most of the trees around the garden are
native or naturalised oaks, chestnuts, limes
and beech.
With a few exceptions planted on pockets of
clay further down the slope all the trees are
relatively drought tolerant species.
Non native trees around the garden include:

Acer monspessulanum
Aesculus flava
Aesculus indica
Aesculus pavia "Atrosanguinea"
Carpinus betulus "Pendula"
Cercidiphyllum japonicum
Cornus mas
Crataegus prunifolia
Crataegus tanaecetifolia
Crataegus x lavallei
Fagus sylvatica "Heterophylla"
Fraxinus americana
Fraxinus angustifolia
Fraxinus excelsior "Jaspidea"
Fraxinus ornus
Fraxinus velutina
Malus baccata "Yellow siberian"
Malus hupehensis
Malus "Red Sentinel"
Malus Transitoria
Parottia persica
Populus nigra "Italica"
Quercus cerris
Quercus ilex
Quercus macranthera
Quercus suber
Quercus x hispanica "Lucombeana"
Zelkova serrata
Zelkova vershaffeltii

Acknowledgments

Above all, we are grateful to Joan and Murray Stuart-Smith who rebuilt the Barn in 1986 when we were in our mid 20's. Very few people have the chance to start on a garden that early in life, let alone manage to stick with it for the next quarter of a century. This would have been impossible without their vision and generosity.
Our thanks also to the great array of family, friends, gardeners and builders who have helped make the garden what it is. Our children Rose, Ben and Harry have painted, mulched, strimmed and animated the place.
Amongst many who have built, gardened and been involved in other ways, special thanks are due to Martin Jennings, Graham Hoyle, Mark Osborne, David Middleditch, Mark Todhunter, Roger Walker, John Lawson, John (Ed) Edwards, Brian Maslin and Janusz Paradowski.
This book began as a talk given by Tom at the 2010 Bath Literary Festival at the invitation of our dear friend James Runcie. Marianne Majerus and Andrew Lawson have seen more sunrises here and taken more photographs of the garden over the years than anyone else and they have very generously made their beautiful pictures available without cost. We are extremely grateful to them.
Finally, our thanks to our friend Luca Puri for the design of this book.

Photographic Acknowledgments

Cover: Marianne Majerus
Marianne Majerus: 24, 32, 33, 34, 35, 39, 42-43, 44, 45, 48, 50, 51, 58, 60, 61, 62, 63, 65, 69, 76, 78
Andrew Lawson: 4-5, 18-19, 20-21, 26-27, 28-29, 40, 46-47, 64, 70, 71, 72-73, 74-75, 79
Joan Stuart-Smith: 12
Sue Stuart-Smith: 11, 12, 16, 17, 22, 25, 30, 52, 53, 54, 55, 56-57, 66, 76
Rose Stuart-Smith: 80-81
Harry Stuart-Smith: 76
Tom Stuart-Smith: 3, 6, 7, 15, 16, 36

All Profits from the sale of this book will be divided between two charities:

The Garden Museum
The Garden Museum is the leading national venue for exhibitions and debate on gardens and garden design. It receives no subsidy from national or local government.
www.gardenmuseum.org.uk

New Ways
New Ways is a remarkable charity supporting health, education, water and agricultural development projects in Africa. The focus is on projects that are sustainable and provide a basis for the long term development of a community or region, mostly in areas that are particularly remote or deprived.
www.newways.org.uk

Enquires relating to this book can be made to info@sergehill.co.uk